The Story of Busta House

Marsali Taylor

Published by lulu.com December 2012

Copyright Marsali Taylor.

All rights reserved.

IBSN 978-1-291-21914-2

I would like to thank Joe and Veronica Rocks, of Busta House Hotel, for their help and encouragement with this pamphlet, and for the use of their photographs. Most of the photographs were taken by Philip Taylor.

A shortened version of this 'Story of Busta House' was printed in *Shetland Life,* November 2011.

This pamphlet is dedicated to the memory of

Elma Johnson

story-teller, guide, folklorist, and an expert on the history of Busta House.

The Story of Busta House

Marsali Taylor

The Story of Busta House

Busta House - the former main entrance, with Thomas and Elizabeth Gifford's arms above the door.

CONTENTS

Early records of Busta and the Giffords p7
Robert Gifford p7
John Gifford p8
Thomas and Elizabeth Gifford p8
Thomas and Elizabeth's first tragedy: the smallpox
.... p13
The arrival of Baabie Pitcairn p15
The deaths of the sons of the house p16
Barbara and John's marriage lines p19
The birth of Gideon, and his adoption by Thomas Gifford
.... p21
Barbara's return to Lerwick, and her life there p23
The deaths of Thomas, Barbara and Lady Busta p25
The certificate of marriage p27
The First Lawsuit, 1832-6 .... p29
Arthur Gifford of Busta's Will p33
The Second Lawsuit, 1923-5 .... p35
Busta House is sold p36
Barbara Pitcairn's Ghost p39

The Story of Busta House

Coming up the steps from the seaward gate towards the oldest part of Busta House,.

The Story of Busta House

Early records of Busta and the Giffords

The first mention of Busta, or 'Bjarstadt', Bjorn's place, is in a deed from 1488, where it's mentioned in the division of the estate of 'younger Hans Sigardson'. In 1545, William the Fowde in 'Brusted' added his seal to a document, and William Sinclair, Foude, granted lands including Busta and Weathersta, on the opposite side of the voe, to the Reverend James Hay, vicar of Unst.

The Gifford family was descended from John Gifford of Sheriffhall, in Midlothian, Scotland. John Gifford, his second son, is recorded as the minister in Northmavine in 1567. His wife, Margaret, was the sister of Sir Patrick Ballenden of Stennis in Orkney, and they had three sons. They were already living in Weathersta, opposite Busta, before 1555, as their son Andrew was born there. John Gifford died before 1577.

Andrew married Agnes Robertson, and they had three children, all born at Weathersta in the early 1570s. In 1583, Andrew bought the lands of Weathersta from the laird, Robert Stewart, Earl of Orkney and Shetland (the half-brother of Mary Queen of Scots). Earl Robert reserved the use of two or three rooms in the manor house on the estate. Andrew's daughter Margaret married Edward Sinclair of Marrister, Whalsay. John, the heir to Weathersta, married Marjory Bruce, and between 1600 and 1620 they had six sons and ten daughters.

Robert Gifford

The original house of Busta dates from 1588, making it the oldest continuously inhabited house in Shetland. It was bought in the 1640s by John's third son, Robert Gifford, first Laird Gifford of Busta. Gifford perhaps moved into Busta House shortly after his marriage to Elizabeth, daughter of Olla Manson of Islesburgh, the neighbouring estate to the north, as their two youngest children were born at Busta.

Robert Gifford's house is the two-storey building with crow-stepped gables – the building on your right that you come into as you enter down the long flight of steps guarded by two gargoyles.

Robert and Elizabeth had only three children, and the two oldest, Laurence and Marjory, both died in their early twenties - Laurence soon after his marriage to Isobel Scollay. Marjory was also married, to the Reverend Hugh Leigh, of Bressay, and died after giving birth to twins. Robert Gifford himself died in 1678, at the age of 73.

John Gifford

John Gifford, Robert's youngest child, was born in 1656, and became his successor as Laird of Busta. He married Agnes Leslie of Tingwall when he was only 22. They had a large family: eight sons and two daughters. The older daughter, Anna, married the Reverend Andrew Fisken, of Delting, and their son John was later to be tutor to the sons of her brother, Thomas. John's fifth son, Andrew, was to buy the Ollaberry estate, just north of Brae.

John Gifford was a person of some importance in the county of Zetland. He was Commissioner of Supply for Zetland for the years 1689, 1690, 1698 and 1704, and was also chamberlain for the Earl of Morton, the chief landowner in the isles. He died in 1705.

Thomas and Elizabeth Gifford

John's oldest son, Robert, died as a teenager, and so it was his second son, Thomas, born around 1680, who inherited the Busta estates. Thomas enlarged the house in 1714 and again in 1720, adding a three-story gable, the part that includes the present bar and the little porch on the sea side. At that time he had just married Elizabeth Mitchell, the daughter of Sir John Mitchell of Westshore, Scalloway. Their arms are in a carved stone panel above the south entrance. He also built a harbour below the house, and set up a fishing station there.

The Story of Busta House

The armorial arms of Thomas Gifford and Elizabeth Mitchell, above the south entrance to the oldest part of Busta House. The motto 'Spare Not' is a shortening of 'Spare when you have Nought'.

There is a good deal of information on Thomas Gifford, for he wrote a 'Historical Description of the Shetland Islands' in 1733, now our main source of information about Shetland at that time. A transcript of his business correspondence for 1744 - 47 also exists. He was the principal merchant and curer in Shetland at the time, trading cargoes of dried salted fish, butter, oil and hosiery in Hamburg, Scotland and Scandinavia.

Thomas was chamberlain to the Earl of Morton, and the Steward-Depute of the Islands. This involved holding a court twice yearly in Lerwick, as well as a circuit court yearly in each parish. He seemed a kindly, principled, religious man, a good husband and father, but he could be ruthless in business, and unprincipled as to how he acquired land. For example, Oliphant of Ure's lands were mortgaged to Gifford. Oliphant was heard drinking a health to Prince Charlie just before the Jacobite rebellion (1745-6), and Gifford blackmailed him into giving over his land, or going to prison. Oliphant took to visiting Busta at night, shouting curses, and after one such visit, in January 1744, he was found dead near Mavis Grind.

The portraits of Thomas and Elizabeth Gifford still hang in the Long Room at Busta. Thomas's portrait makes him look rather severe, a magistrate who would not let anyone off lightly. The companion portrait of his wife, known as Madam Busta, is more appealing; she looks young and uncertain, her hair fashionably powdered grey, her big eyes staring out at the observer. A handful of letters from her are extant, but the real source for her character comes from memories of her given by witnesses at the court proceedings of 1832. Almost all witnesses agree she was a very proud and violent-tempered lady, very determined in her purpose, not easily reconciled where she had taken offence, "and could bear contradiction from no-one," said Mrs Janet Sinclair, who stayed twice at Busta in the 1760s, "but she was a bright woman, and could have been the first duchess in the land. Her appearance commanded respect from everyone."

John Cheyne, of Tangwick, whose mother was Thomas's niece, told a story of a card game called 'catch the ten': "other players strove not to hold the ten, or to throw it in [Lady Busta's] way, while if she held it, they endeavored to avoid taking it, in order to prevent a quarrel with her, and that he heard his mother say, she was often much difficulted how to avoid taking Lady Busta's ten."

The Story of Busta House

The portraits of Thomas and Elizabeth Gifford, which still hang in the Long Room at Busta House.

The Story of Busta House

Thomas and Elizabeth's first tragedy: the smallpox

Elizabeth Mitchell was only in her late teens when she and Thomas were married, and she had fourteen children in the next nineteen years. Unusually, only one died as an infant, but in November 1740 tragedy struck the family, with the children coming down with smallpox. Thomas's diary entry is sad reading:

'18 [December] My dear Betty died about 7 at night in a very calm manner. Robbie lay all that day. 19 Wednesday. Poor Frankie died about 7 at night, very calm. 21 The pox began to appear on Robbie and Christie, and they lay all that day. The bairns were buried. Anderina took the bed. 25 Tuesday. Hay took ye bed, all the bairns uneasy, but blessed be God, not very ill.'

Robbie, Christie and Anderina recovered, but Thomas and Elizabeth's second son James, 9-year-old Barbara, and their youngest child, Thomas, were all to die within the next months.

There was a more cheerful time in 1744, when their oldest daughter Margaret married William Neven from Windhouse, Yell. According to Gifford's correspondence, his oldest sons John and Robert were away at this time, supervising his voyages and collecting monies due to him.

The Story of Busta House

The arrival of Baabie Pitcairn

At some point before 1747, two gentlewomen in their early twenties came to stay with Elizabeth Gifford. They were Barbara, or Baabie, and Alice Pitcairn, sisters of good family, but not wealthy. Their father was George Pitcairn, a brother of Pitcairn of Muness, a Lerwick merchant and captain of his own trading vessel; their mother was Ursula Bruce, who lived in one of the largest houses in Lerwick.

The sisters were treated as part of the family. According to Thomas Gifford's ledger, they shared the services of "a Dancing Master, Wm Troup", with his own children. If there were impromptu dances in the evening, no doubt the older brothers and the two Pitcairn girls would have danced together.

Robert Ridland, who saw her in Lerwick when he was a boy, described Barbara Pitcairn as "a pretty and lady-looking woman". She was, he said, "companion and gentlewoman to Lady Busta, and next in consequence to her". John, the heir to Busta, now thirty-one, and still unmarried, was said to have told his mother that "he would marry Barbara Pitcairn in spite of the world." She retorted that she would rather see him "dead at her feet than married to Baabie Pitcairn."

She was to have her wish.

The deaths of the sons of the house

On Saturday, 14th May, 1748, in the afternoon, the four sons of the house set out to visit their cousins at Weathersta, along with the younger boys' tutor, their cousin Reverend John Fisken. Fisken was currently his father's assistant in Northmavine, but about to take over Tingwall Parish. There was also a grieve to handle the boat. They did not return.

We have no contemporary account of the accident. There is a poem in the Shetland Museum and Archives, tentatively dated to the 1750s, titled, *Upon the sudden, surprising and most Lamentable death of the Messrs John, Robert, William and Hay Gifford of Busta, and Mr John Fisken, Preacher of the gospel, and Magnus Johnson, Servant, who all perished by sea twixt Busta and Weathersta, 14th May 1748*. It's believed to be by Reverend Andrew Fisken, John's father. It gives no details of the accident, but eulogizes the young men in flowery terms:

> *Worthy John Gifford, mainstay of the name,*
> *Northmavine ought to register his fame*
> *In Marble Tables with an Iron Pen,*
> *And sign him what he was, a man of men.*
> *His Learning, wisdom and his Eloquence,*
> *His kindness, prudence and benevolence,*
> *His justice and his works of charity,*
> *Will will his name to perpetuity.*
> *In th'other three although their years was green,*
> *The buds of virtue to spring forth was seen,*
> *As for the preacher, lovely Mr John,*
> *None who heard him but will his loss bemoan,*
> *His heavn'n spring gifts stand not in need of proctors,*
> *Which made him fit to sit among the Doctors.*

If the 1750s dating is accurate, this is the only near-contemporary record of who was lost, and when, for none of the 1832 court case witnesses could remember the tragedy personally, and differed in details as to which bodies were found. One added a boy from the estate to the deaths, and another called the grieve John Manson, probably correctly, for she knew his son - the Shetland patronymic system tended to cause confusion among Scottish residents.

Traditionally, it was a calm, fine night, but there's no mention of the weather in the records. Mrs Janet Sinclair spoke of the boat being driven on shore, with Mr John's stick and dog in the stern; all other accounts spoke of the boat being "upset".

On Monday morning, boats from Delting and Northmavine were set to drag the voe. It was Lawrence Johnston's father who found the body of John Gifford – "the dredge took hold of his thumb." They knew from John's watch what time the accident had occurred: "it had stopped at 12 o clock." Some witnesses said the grieve's body had also been found, and two thought Robert, the second son, had been washed up in Orkney.

Nobody ever knew what had happened that night. Mrs Elizabeth Ross, whose mother was connected to Lady Busta, had heard that John Gifford thought Mr Fisken was also courting Barbara Pitcairn, and suggested he and John had quarrelled over John's behaviour to her. This is reasonable enough; if they were unmarried, John was acting badly by a young gentlewoman, his mother's guest, and if they were married, it was time he summoned up the courage to declare her as his wife. Mrs Ross thought that they had fought, upsetting the boat.

Another suggestion was that the men were involved in a drunken accident. It was a hard-drinking age, they had been at their cousins' house all afternoon, and were returning late, so it's an entirely plausible suggestion.

Tradition invokes the supernatural. According to *Annals of the Parish*, by P W Greig (1892), the boys had had an excursion to Hillswick the day before, to shoot seals. On the way home, the boat's keel was gripped, as if from below, and the boat only moved forward after Mr Fisken knelt in prayer – when three dark, seal-like creatures were seen to move slowly, reluctantly, back from the boat. This incident frightened the youngest boy, Hay, enough to take his pony the next day, rather than cross by boat. He wanted to ride home, but someone had untied his pony, and so he got into the boat with the others. That's all rather sinister: the missing pony that meant all four sons of the house had to return by boat, the calm night when no accident should have occurred... It makes you want to ask who benefited from their deaths, or what enemies Thomas Gifford had - the sons of Olliphant of Ure, for example, who only four years earlier had shouted out that Gifford would have no heirs to his house.

The pier and beach below Busta House.

The Story of Busta House

Barbara and John's Marriage Lines

John's body was taken to Busta pier. The traditional version of the story continues that Baabie Pitcairn ran to the body, stooped over it and took a paper from the inside pocket – her marriage lines. Then she broke the news to Lady Busta that she was John's widow, and the mother-to-be of his son.

Now the witnesses become divided. A number said they had heard nothing of any paper found on John Gifford's body. Others mentioned a letter to Miss Henderson, the girl Lady Busta wanted him to marry. Mrs Ross had heard of a paper: "It was dried and given to Lady Busta." Lawrence Johnston said he'd been told that when they took the body to the pier, then Barbara Pitcairn came out, and said, "That's the body, and I am five months gone with child to that body." She stated they'd been privately married by Mr Fisken. Johnston had heard the marriage had taken place at Marrister, on the island of Whalsay, on the 1st of April 1748. Christian Gifford, now Lady Symbister, the wife of Whalsay's principal landowner, had been visiting her parents at Busta, and John Gifford, Robert and Barbara Pitcairn had accompanied her home.

Miss Craigie Sinclair, who'd lived as companion with her aunt Lady Ure, another sister of Lady Busta, also believed in a private marriage at Symbister House. She'd heard from her aunt that the paper found on the body was marriage lines, which were shown to Lady Busta. Johnston had heard that the paper was "from Barbara Pitcairn to John Gifford, and showed she was with child by him on the head of marriage – all the papers on the body were shown to Lady Busta." Janet Murray, a servant at Lunna in the 1850s, had heard Barbara had written lines of marriage – "if she'd not had these to be shown, the boy would not be admitted to be John Gifford's child."

Others said that they had heard that Barbara alleged only that John had given her a promise of marriage, "but," said Mrs Jean Tarrel, who had been a teenager when Barbara visited her parents in Lerwick, "she was a lady of honour, and would not have alleged a promise of marriage unless it had been true."

Lady Busta was furious, and determined that the despised dependent would not take her place as mistress of Busta. "She wouldn't allow her to take the name of Gifford," Mrs Ross said. Miss

19

The Story of Busta House

Craigie Sinclair remembered that Lady Ure "had not been pleased with the way Lady Busta had behaved to Miss Pitcairn about the marriage." Another witness had heard of Lady Busta stealing Barbara's papers from her trunk, and destroying them.

"The lady was provoked at her for presuming to say that John Gifford had promised to marry her – she was a high-minded person, and had a great deal of family pride," said the Reverend Peter Barclay, son of the minister of Delting.

The birth of John and Barbara's son, Gideon, and his adoption by Thomas Gifford

Mr Barclay had heard that Barbara had left Busta before her son was born, as had the Reverend William Jack, later to be that child's tutor. Lawrence Johnston had heard the child was born in a garret. However, Mrs Ross said that at the birth, Lady Busta sent attendance, and everything else required. Mrs Jean Tulloch, whose father was from Weathersta, said that the boy was born "at Busta, in what was called the South Ha', being a small house adjoining to the big house ... part of the house of Busta, but entered by a separate entrance." The date was 6 November 1748.

Barbara Tait's father and brother were both at Busta at the time the sons were drowned. "When the young woman was kythed with child," she deposed, "and charged therewith before the minister and elders, she gave in the name of the eldest son, John Gifford, as the father of the child, and that Lady Busta could not bear to hear it alleged that her son 'aught' the child, and that after this Lady Busta had a dream in which her son appeared to her, and told her that the child was his, and ordered her to take care of it. In consequence Lady Busta took the child and put it to nurse."

Robert Ridland said that Mrs Scott of Lund had visited the child and told her sister, Lady Busta, that it was very like John, and that was what had induced her to take it.

The child was christened at Busta House, in the presence of the servants, and treated thereafter as the grandson of the house, and Thomas's heir to the Busta estates.

However, his legitimacy was still in doubt. A letter from Thomas Gifford to his lawyer made it clear that he thought Gideon was not legitimate, speaking only of a possible intention of marriage: "... my eldest son .. left a girl with child. Whether he designed [meant] to marry her or not, I know not." He also made out a bond for £10,000 in Gideon's favour, as his alternative inheritance if his will was set aside because of Gideon's illegitimacy.

When he was eleven, Gideon gained company at Busta House. His aunt Andrina, who had married her cousin Patrick Gifford of Ollaberry in 1750 or 51, died in 1759, leaving three young children:

The Story of Busta House

Andrew, aged seven, and his younger brother and sister, Thomas and Elizabeth. Madam Busta took the children into her household on the death of their mother. Their father died in that same year. If Gideon had not been preferred, then Andrew would have been the heir to the Busta estate, and no doubt as he grew up he would have been aware of this. There's a suggestion that even then Andrew wasn't a completely reliable character, as he was sent abroad at a young age, probably by Madam Busta, in which case it would have been before he was seventeen. It was a common way of 'disposing' of an unsatisfactory family member, and the statement that he lost his property in America in the War of Independence suggests that he was given money to set himself up there. You wonder if perhaps, while Gideon was studying at University, he spoke once too often, or in Madam Busta's presence, about how the estates should have come to him.

There's a visible reminder of Gideon's youth in the present-day house. In the Bigga room, part of the wall is rough plaster; on it, behind glass, is a clear signature, 'Gideon Gifford Esq of Busta.' The landing just outside, above the entrance, where the rocking horse stands, was once a child's room.

Gideon Gifford's signature in the Bigga Room.

Barbara's return to Lerwick, and her life there

Tradition has Barbara Pitcairn remaining at Busta House, and being treated as a servant by Lady Busta, but this does not seem to have been the case. Barbara left Busta House, "too soon after her confinement, in consequence of a quarrel with Lady Busta," Robert Ridland said, and returned to her mother's house in Lerwick, now 97 Commercial Street. She lived there until her death on 5th May 1766, and so the court records have a number of first-hand witnesses to her life there. She was known as a fine knitter and spinner, and, several people said, "much respected". She was supported in part from the Busta estate, with a fat cow at Hallowmas, and a lispund of wool at Lammas.

Mrs Jean Tarrel remembered Barbara visiting her parents when she herself was a teenager: she wore "a fine yellow silk gown, with a white flowered and laced apron, and excessive fine lace on her cap, fine handkerchief and ruffles, and elegantly dressed."

Barbara McClellan was also a teenager when she ran errands to Barbara's house for her mother: she "remembered her in printed cambric or white cambric. She had a delicate and rather melancholy look, and was very much reserved."

The Story of Busta House

97, Commercial Street, Lerwick, where Barbara Pitcairn lived.

The deaths of Thomas, Barbara and Lady Busta

Barbara Pitcairn saw her son only once more, in 1762 or 3, when he was around 16, and visiting Lerwick on his way to study further in Aberdeen. Thomas Gifford had died in 1760, and Gideon had inherited the estate of Busta, although Lady Busta continued to run it. He was then grown to be a fine young man, praised by his tutors for his application and amiable disposition. He was 18 when his mother died; her funeral was paid by the Busta estate.

Lady Busta died three years after Barbara Pitcairn, in 1769. Of her fourteen children, only Christian, Lady Symbister, had outlived her.

Gideon Gifford of Busta.

The certificate of marriage

Now the story takes a strange twist. Gideon Gifford lived on at Busta, with, apparently, the consent of all the family. He had one son, James, born in 1771, by Margaret Sutherland - nothing more is known about her. Gideon married Grizel Nicolson in 1773, and they seem to have had a long and happy marriage. They had eight children, and six lived to adulthood. The oldest daughters, Elizabeth and Grace, did not marry. Gideon's oldest son, Arthur, had two illegitimate children, Gideon and Jessie, but his marriage to Mary Hay was childless. The next daughter, Jessie, married John Scott of Scalloway, and they had five children. Christian married the Reverend William Langridge, the Methodist minister, and they had two daughters. Thomas had a son, Thomas, by a twenty-year old servant girl, Agnes Jamieson; he then married Jessie Scott, of Melby, and they had eight children. After the tragedy, the Gifford family seemed to be thriving.

Then, in the 1790s, Lady Symbister was alleged to have found a packet wrapped in coarse paper in an old chest which had belonged to Lady Busta. Inside was a certificate of marriage between John and Barbara, and a letter from her mother, expressing her regret for having concealed the truth, and asking her to publicize Gideon's legitimacy. Lady Symbister called her servants together and announced the news that her brother had married Barbara Pitcairn. She then put the certificate back in a secret drawer, and said no more about it before her death in 1799.

The certificate of marriage appeared again in January 1803, in the hands of Andrew Gifford of Ollaberry, the boy who had grown up at Busta with his older cousin Gideon. He had returned from America to Ollaberry, probably in the late 1770s. He set up a fish curing business there, and married Gideon's wife's sister Andrina in 1783. Generally, the two men were on good terms. Andrew had a large family - five sons, five daughters - and Gideon helped him financially and in kind - in a later settlement, there is talk of a gift of fowls and mutton, and the payment of a school bill.

According to Andrew, he found the certificate in a secret drawer in a chest of the late Lady Symbister. His letter enclosed a copy, and a request for that Gideon make over to him two small parts of the Busta estate, which it seems Gideon had said he would give him (we only have Andrew's word for this) and not ask for any rents Andrew had already received from them. Gideon refused to be blackmailed, and Andrew's next letter, in 1804, announced that he had lost the certificate. In 1805, he wrote to Gideon's agent, saying that it was not lost after all, and enclosing the original. It said:

> *At Busta, 8th December 1747. These certify, that this day, John Gifford of Busta, younger, and Barbara Pitcairn, there, were duly married in presence of William Gifford and Hay Gifford, his brothers, by*
>
> JOHN FISKEN ,
> *Minr.*
>
> WILLM GIFFORD, *Witness.*
> HAY GIFFORD, *Witness.*

In 1808, Andrew wrote to Gideon again, threatening to start proceedings against him, on the grounds that he was not the lawful heir, and a number of letters passed between Andrew and Gideon and his son Arthur. Gideon insisted that Andrew owed him £300, but seemed willing to come to terms rather than go to law. At one point Andrew accepted the offer of an annuity of £25, but the agreement was broken when Gideon raised a summons against him for the £300.

In May 1810, Andrew gathered together a number of gentlemen at his house, and swore an affidavit that the certificate he had produced was forged by him, at the instigation of Gideon Gifford – a charge which Gideon promptly denied, saying, 'Then Ollaberry may say what he pleases.' Andrew died shortly afterwards, and both Gideon and his wife died a year later, in 1811.

The First Lawsuit, 1832-6

There was peace at Busta for another twenty years. Gideon's older son, Arthur, took over the Busta estate, and made annuity payments to Mrs Andrina Gifford of Ollaberry, to help her in bringing up her children. All her daughters had survived, but she now had only one son living. Arthur Gifford of Ollaberry was a Purser in the Royal Navy, and living in York, Upper Canada. When his mother died in 1830, he came home, and it was said that reading her letters determined him on bringing a case against Arthur of Busta for possession of the estate. He was not well off, and his three brothers-in-law helped finance the case, to their loss. Andrew Duncan, his sister Catherine's husband, was a well-known lawyer and WS in Lerwick, and he acted for Arthur of Ollaberry in absentia - Ollaberry had returned to Canada, where his two daughters were born, Andrina in 1832 and Christina in 1834.

The case was heard in February 1832. The Commission which investigated it interviewed over fifty witnesses here in Shetland – the men and women I've quoted. The jury found in favour of Gideon's son as lawful heir of Busta.

Arthur of Ollaberry appealed, and the case came up before Lord Cockburn, at the Court of Sessions. The case was heard over the winter, and decision was finally given in 1836. Summing up, Lord Cockburn was very critical of Andrew Gifford of Ollaberry, and hence of the certificate he produced, listing his record of assertion and denial, and stating that there was no proof that the certificate was found as he said. He called the certificate itself 'extremely suspicious', pointing out that the signature of William Gifford differed in three ways from other signatures by him. The certificate was dated 'Busta', when the marriage was said to have taken place at Symbister. Furthermore, a certificate did not prove a marriage, and this marriage was unusual in other ways – no banns had been called, because of the objections of the relations of the couple, and it was signed only by the minister and the witnesses, his pupils, boys of seventeen and fourteen.

Other reasons Lord Cockburn gave for disbelieving in the marriage was that witnesses were divided as to whether there had been a marriage; that Barbara had never taken the name of Mrs Gifford, nor conducted herself as a widow, for example by wearing mourning; that Thomas, in his will, had made it clear he thought Gideon illegitimate; and that Gideon himself had never taken any steps to contest the general opinion that he was illegitimate.

The verdict cannot have satisfied either man. Lord Cockburn felt it was up to Arthur of Busta to prove his legitimate descent from John Gifford, and that he had not done this, and so had no automatic right to the estate. However he ruled that old Thomas's Deed of Entail was valid, giving Arthur of Busta the Busta estate, but that Arthur of Ollaberry was entitled to the parts of the estate not included in Thomas's Deed. He gave the costs of the case to Arthur of Busta.

Arthur of Busta appealed against Lord Cockburn's decision, but the appeal was rejected. Arthur of Ollaberry never took possession of the lands awarded to him, but remained in Canada, where he died, in Hamilton, Ontario, in 1844.

The Story of Busta House

Arthur Gifford of Busta.

The Story of Busta House

Arthur of Busta's sister, Jessie, who married John Scott of Scalloway.

Thomas Gifford, younger brother of Arthur of Busta.

Arthur Gifford of Busta's Will

The expenses awarded against Arthur of Busta had crippled the once wealthy house - he died over £30,000 in debt. The only male Gifford of the next generation, his brother Thomas's son, Gideon, had died in 1853, so Arthur had no obvious heir. He did not get on well with Thomas's widow and her other daughters, but gave Thomas's youngest daughter, Thomasina, the rights that her brother Gideon would have had: an allowance of £100 a year, and a suite of rooms at Busta. The terms of his will were that the estate would be put in the hands of trustees who would work to clear the debt as soon as possible without selling parts of the estate. Once the debts were paid, the estate was to be made over to the next male heir, from a list of the children of his sisters; after them came his own natural daughter, Jessie, and her daughter, Jane Sinclair. If there were no male heirs of any of these, the estate could go personally or to the male heirs of Arthur of Ollaberry's two daughters in Canada, or, failing them, to the two elder sons of his lawyer, Henry Cheyne, of Tangwick. Failing these, the estate was to go to any heirs whatsoever. A number of female relatives were left annuities. His widow was one of the trustees. His niece Thomasina Gifford retained her 'living rights' at Busta, and could appoint one trustee.

Arthur of Busta died in 1856. Now, after the large families of the previous generation, it seemed that Oliphant of Ure's curse that there would not be an heir for Busta, had returned to haunt them. Of the thirteen relatives named, only two had children: Arthur's sister Jessie's son, Gideon Scott, had two daughters, Grace and Frances, and his sister Christian's daughter, Grace Henwood, had a daughter, Christina Jane. These three women, Arthur's great-nieces, were to become 'the Ladies of Busta' in the 1925 lawsuit. Arthur of Ollaberry's daughters could not be traced. John Cheyne of Tangwick applied for the estate in 1897, but was refused on the grounds that the debt was not yet paid off, and he too died childless.

In her account, *The True Romance of Busta*, Frances Scott is bitter against the trustees. She alleges that the annuities were not paid for long, and that several of the recipients died in poverty. Tomasina, particularly, was not allowed to keep her rooms at Busta, nor to appoint a trustee to defend her rights. No real and active steps,

Frances Scott later alleged, had been made to clear the debt, although the estate made enough money for more land to be bought. By the end of seventy years, the £30,000 had been reduced by only £5,000. There is certainly a local tradition that the debt could have been paid off, but that the trustees didn't wish to relinquish the estate.

Immediately after Arthur's death, the house was lived in by Arthur's brother Thomas's illegitimate son, known as Thomas Factor, who died in October, 1899. From the early twentieth century, Busta house was inhabited by Arthur 'Ertie' White, the estate factor, his wife Rosa and their children. The trustees continued to run the estate, and the £4,000 fund *in medio* had grown to £7,000 (through unauthorized sales of land, according to Frances Scott) by 1925.

In World War I, Busta was used as a naval headquarters. The surrounding waters of Swarbacks Minn made a sheltered anchorage, protected by the huge guns which still jut out from their emplacements on the island of Vementry. At one point, after the sinking of the *Royal Oak* in Orkney, much of the British fleet was in Shetland. There was a fuelling depot opposite Busta house, at Weathersta. Busta House itself was the home of Rear Admiral W B Fawckner, in command of the 10th Cruiser Squadron. It was at this time that the pier was given a wooden extension.

The Second Lawsuit, 1923-5

The second lawsuit over the House of Busta began when Jane Sinclair, the last of the people whose 'male heirs' had been designated as successors, died unmarried in 1921. This meant that the 'heirs whatsoever' could now put in a claim, and Arthur Gifford's three remaining great-nieces did so.

The suit came before the court in 1923. In June 1925, Lord Morison in the Court of Sessions ruled that Grace Scott, Frances Scott and Christina Henwood, the 'Ladies of Busta', were entitled to the Estate of Busta as Arthur Gifford's 'heirs whatsoever', and sisted [delayed] the process of transferring the estate for six months to allow the heirs and trustees to come to terms. On 15th December 1925, Lord Morison confirmed his judgement, and ordered the trustees (named as John Cook, WS, Edinburgh, and another) to hand over the estate, under the burden of debt. According to Frances Scott, the trustees then invoked second *Bondholders in Possession* and brought in an action for *Maills and Duties*, retaining power over the estate, and forbidding the Ladies to take even moveable items from the house by the threat of poinding on the ground. The Ladies lived for a short time at 'The Booth', under conditions of great hardship, according to Frances Scott, but never succeeded in entering the House itself.

Busta House is sold

The debt was finally paid off during World War II, with the income from quarrying stone for Scatsta airstrip, and Busta House was sold in the 1940s. The new owner was Captain Macgregor.

The second owner of Busta was Sir Basil Neven-Spence. Sir Basil's family had been in Shetland for many years - his father was Thomas Spence of Gardiesfield, Unst. Sir Basil lived for some time in the Haa on the Unst isle of Uyea - his three children were born there. He had been an army medical officer, serving in the Middle East, and then at Aldershot. He retired with the rank of Major in 1927, and became Vice-Convener of the Zetland County Council. He stood for election as the Conservative MP for Orkney and Shetland in 1929, stepped down as a candidate in 1931, and was elected in 1935. He served as MP until 1950. He was knighted in 1945, and made Vice-Lieutenant of Scotland. He was Lord Lieutenant of Shetland for many years, and, as photos in the Long Room show, the Queen and Duke of Edinburgh visited him at Busta in the 1960s. It was he who brought the House of Commons gargoyles to guard the entrance steps - they had been damaged in the war, and were to be thrown away. Sir Basil kept the house as his Shetland home until his death, in 1974.

Sir Basil Neven-Spence with Her Majesty Queen Elizabeth II, during her visit to Shetland.

The Story of Busta House

The Story of Busta House

Busta House became a hotel in 1976, under the ownership of Peter Watts. It was expanded by Mr and Mrs Cope in 1983-4 - the new piece of the house is the wing nearest the main road, the part of the house which includes the present restaurant and the rooms above. It has been owned by Joe and Veronica Rocks since January 2000. Under their ownership, Busta has become a popular place to stop for afternoon tea in the Long Room, or to go for a evening meal. They also host special occasions: for our wedding in 2001, my husband and I took all the assembled family members for a meal there, followed by an evening in the Long Room, under the gaze of the portraits of Thomas and Madam Busta, where the late Elma Johnson told us the story of the Tragedy of Busta.

The Long Room

The Story of Busta House

Barbara Pitcairn's Ghost

What about one of Shetland's best-known ghost stories, the tradition that Barbara Pitcairn haunts Busta House?

Well, the website Shetlopedia takes the story of Busta House from *Grant's County Families of Shetland* and inserts, between the story of John's death and the entry on Gideon, "It is said that Elizabeth died of grief, and that her ghost still roams Busta House. When she died in 1769, just one daughter of all her fourteen children was still living." The second sentence makes it clear that Elizabeth isn't a mistake for Barbara – and when you think about it, Lady Busta is a much more likely ghost. She has all the elements for an unquiet shade: the bitter resentment in life, her ill-treatment of Barbara and the tragic loss of so many of her children. Furthermore, Busta was her house – who has a better right to haunt it?

The original of *Grant's County Families*, also on Shetlopedia, doesn't mention a ghost. Nor, more significantly, does Greig's *Annals of the Parish*, which devotes two chapters to the Busta story, and digresses with a number of folklore traditions. If the ghost had been known then, I'm sure Greig would have mentioned her.

Interestingly, it doesn't seem to have been widely known in Sir Basil's time either. Elsie Wood from Muckle Roe worked in Busta House then.

"It was my first job," she told me. "I was just a young girl, fifteen, and I'd never heard anything about it. It was a spooky house though, especially at night, with the moon shining in all the little windows – if I had to get up at night, I'd wake Kathleen, who worked with me, to come along. I certainly never saw a ghost, or heard strange noises, or anything like that."

"It was only after I'd worked there I heard about the ghost, and then Kathleen said, 'Well maybe that was why the dog wouldn't go in that room. It was supposed to be the room Barbara Pitcairn had, a room past where we slept. Sir Basil had a black Labrador, and it wouldn't go in there."

Joe Rocks, the present owner, thinks he first heard of a ghost in the 1980s. "The owners were marketing the house a bit more then. However, there have been a number of instances of strange things happening, from the late 1980s, when Mr and Mrs Jones owned the hotel. They spoke of electrical disturbances, and laundry being folded. There was a minister visiting, and he complained of a smell in the room. They moved him, and the same happened the next night, but the third room was in the new wing, and that was fine."

Joe took me upstairs to the Gifford Library, a calm room with a bonny view out over the voe, and a welcoming fire. On the wall are the portraits of Arthur Gifford and two of his sisters. "When we first came here, for the first two years, I was always conscious of an atmosphere here, a chill, and a distinctive smell, not unpleasant – a perfume, almost as if someone had just sprayed 'Haze' in the room. It was floral, a bit like lavender, I suppose."

How about sightings of Barbara Pitcairn herself?

"The lady was seen in 2005 by one of our workers tidying up in the dining room," Joe told me. "She'd finished the settings, and switched the lights off - except that they wouldn't go out. She went to look for a master switch, and when she came back, around the corner, a lady dressed in brown hessian, sackcloth-like material, was sitting at the back of the room, with two glasses crossed on the floor by her. The girl screamed, and ran as fast as she could, and our manager came. He didn't see the lady, she was gone, but he saw the crossed glasses."

The electrical disturbances at Busta House continue. "One night," Joe said, "at 1.30am, my light began flashing on, a gentle flash, every 25 or 30 seconds. I was tired, so I just rolled over and went to sleep. However, six months later, when we had the media conference for Atlantic Airways here, then I mentioned this to the PR people at dinner, and one of them came down the next morning saying that his light-bulb had done this too. We all went and looked, and of course it was fine. He had his breakfast, went back up, then came back to say, quietly, that it was doing it again. We looked, and saw it too. The odd thing was, that that was in the 1983 part of the house, as is the restaurant and the laundry – but then, we don't know what outbuildings might have been here in Barbara Pitcairn's time."

The Story of Busta House

Who knows? Perhaps this was where the South Ha' was, where Gideon was born, and that's why the tradition is that it's the ghost of poor Barbara, looking for the son that proud Lady Busta took from her...

The Story of Busta House

Also by Marsali Taylor:

Women's Suffrage in Shetland

Only a small society on a distant group of islands - yet the women in Shetland's Suffrage societies were fully in touch with the national movement. Visiting speakers included Crystal Macmillan and Dr Elsie Inglis, and the president of the 1909 Society marched with Mrs Pankhurst. In researching her own local societies, Taylor gives a history of the whole Suffrage movement from its formal beginnings in the 1840s to women's work in World War I. She follows the long-fought battle for equal treatment within marriage, and fair pay and working conditions, University education and greater involvement in the running of state institutions.

'Splendid - an indication of how much more there can be done in the field of women's history in Shetland.' Angus Johnston, Archives Assistant, Shetland Museum and Archives.

' ... brimful with details culled from newspapers, archive material and interviews with descendents ... It shows what can be achieved by researching a topic such as female suffrage within a relatively small and isolated community. It is clearly a labour of love, and this reviewer enjoyed it very much.' Alison McCall, *History Scotland.*

Death on a Longship

When she wangles the job of skippering a Viking longship for a film, Cass Lynch thinks her big break has finally arrived - even though it means returning home to the Shetland Islands, which she ran away from as a teenager. Then the 'accidents' begin - and when a dead woman turns up on the boat's deck, Cass realises that she, her family and her past are under suspicion from the disturbingly shrewd Detective Inspector Macrae.

Cass must call on all her local knowledge, the wisdom she didn't realise she'd gained from sailing and her glamorous French opera singer mother to clear them all of suspicion - and to catch the killer before Cass becomes the next victim.

You cannot go wrong with this delight of mystery! ... I love it when authors keep things current and relevant to today's issues as well as presenting us with a mystery to solve. **Mysteries etc blog**

The murder mystery element is entirely satisfactory with a few twists along the way that kept me guessing as to who and why. ... I recommend it for anyone who likes an atmospheric, character based mystery - I'm already looking forward to the next in the series. **Hayley Anderton,** *Desperate Reader*

As a detective novel, Death on a Longship is a solid, well-plotted book, with likeable characters. However, what really elevates it above the average murder mystery is the setting. The book takes place almost entirely in Shetland, and the author beautifully evokes the landscape, the people and the language. ... the descriptions of these complex islands are fascinating. The book is as much about Cassandre's uneasy relationship with Shetland as it is about solving a murder - and so the islands' history, culture, dialect, wild beauty, and considerable natural resources, all form part of the story.

I very much enjoyed the book, and would certainly recommend it. The one warning is that, by the end, you may suffer from a burning desire to acquire a boat and sail to Shetland yourself... **L Roberts,** *Amazon*

The Story of Busta House

The Story of Busta House